Pet Names and Numerology

Choose the Right Name for Your Pet

Amy Morford

I dedicate this to pet lovers everywhere who want to better understand their animals.

Copyright © 2014 by Speedy Publishing LLC

All rights reserved. No part of this publication may be reproduced, distributed or transmitted in any form or by any means, including photocopying, recording, or other electronic or mechanical methods, without the prior written permission of the publisher, except in the case of brief quotations embodied in critical reviews and certain other noncommercial uses permitted by copyright law. For permission requests, write to the publisher, addressed "Attention: Permissions Coordinator," at the address below.

Speedy Publishing LLC (c) 2014
40 E. Main St., #1156
Newark, DE 19711
www.speedypublishing.co

Ordering Information:
Quantity sales; Special discounts are available on quantity purchases by corporations, associations, and others. For details, contact the "Special Sales Department" at the address above.

-- 1st edition

Manufactured in the United States of America

Table of Contents

Publisher's Notes i

Chapter 1: Introduction to Numerology 1

Chapter 2: A Brief History 3

Chapter 3: How Pet Numerology Works 4

Chapter 4: How to Analyze Your Pet's Name 5

Chapter 5: Personality Number Interpretations 6

Chapter 6: Master Numbers 13

Chapter 7: Instinctive Reaction Number Interpretations 14

Bonus Chapter: Astrology and Your Pet 16

Meet the Author 21

More Books by Amy Morford 22

Charts 23

Publisher's Notes

Disclaimer

This publication is intended to provide helpful and informative material. It is not intended to diagnose, treat, cure, or prevent any health problem or condition, nor is intended to replace the advice of a physician. No action should be taken solely on the contents of this book. Always consult your physician or qualified health-care professional on any matters regarding your health and before adopting any suggestions in this book or drawing inferences from it.

The author and publisher specifically disclaim all responsibility for any liability, loss or risk, personal or otherwise, which is incurred as a consequence, directly or indirectly, from the use or application of any contents of this book.

Any and all product names referenced within this book are the trademarks of their respective owners. None of these owners have sponsored, authorized, endorsed, or approved this book.

Always read all information provided by the manufacturers' product labels before using their products. The author and publisher are not responsible for claims made by manufacturers.

Print Edition 2014

Chapter 1: Introduction to Numerology

Numerology is the study of information and symbolism about life through numbers.

Numerology has been around for at least 2,500 years. You may be discovering numerology for the first time but it is not a fad and it is not new.

Numerology can be used for all areas of your life and it can be applied to pets. Analyzing a pet name using numerology will provide a blueprint of the animal's personality, strengths and weaknesses.

Your pet's personality can be influenced by what you name it. Their natural temperament will count for approximately 70% and the name you choose will count for approximately 30%.

PET NAMES & NUMEROLOGY

Pet Names and Numerology will focus on helping you pick a pet name with the desired energy best suited for you, or help you understand your current pet's personality and character better.

Let's get started!

CHAPTER 2: A BRIEF HISTORY

The roots of numerology can be traced back to Pythagoras, a Greek mathematician who was born in about 570 B.C. and is a historical figure. Pythagoras developed many of the basic theorems that form the foundation of modern mathematics such as the science of geometry, the formula for a triangle and he is credited with creating the Pythagoras Number System and the science of numerology.

Pythagorean Theorem

Pythagoras was a mathematician, philosopher, theorist and the first person to believe that numbers are the foundation of the universe. All things seen and unseen could be reduced to numbers. During Pythagoras lifetime it was widely accepted that the universe was created from vibrating energy. Pythagoras believed that the characteristics of this vibrating energy could be understood through numbers and that each number had its own vibration. Pythagoras taught that each number had a quality that was unique. To understand the qualities of a person, place or thing, one would simply need to know which numbers made up its vibrating energy.

Chapter 3: How Pet Numerology Works

All things in the universe vibrate at its own frequency. Find the vibration rate of any object and you can establish the qualities and energies associated with it. You can unlock the major frequencies of people and pets by applying the principles of numerology and basic information.

Just like people, animals create a psychological profile through hearing their names. The personality of a pet can be influenced by what you call it. Names have certain characteristics and when you name your pets, they take on the energy of those characteristics.

Chapter 4: How to Analyze Your Pet's Name

The numerology calculation for a pet is simple. All you need is your pet's name. If your pet is titled, registered or has papers, it may have an "official" name. Forget the fancy titles and analyze the name you use on a daily basis. The exception to this rule is nicknames. Many of us have nicknames for our pets. First analyze your pet's "everyday" name and then play around with their nicknames.

The name of your pet should be analyzed in two ways:

1. Personality - The sum of all letters in the name.
2. Instinctive Reaction - The first vowel of a name.

In numerology for animals, we must break down names and convert them into numbers. All numbers are added together until reduced to single digits 1 through 9. The numbers 1, 2, 3, 4, 5, 6, 7, 8, and 9 represent the major vibration rates associated with people and animals' characteristics.

To convert names into numbers we will use Pythagoras' system for assigning a number to each letter of the alphabet. Below is The Pythagorean System.

PYTHAGOREAN NUMBER SYSTEM

1	2	3	4	5	6	7	8	9
A	B	C	D	E	F	G	H	I
J	K	L	M	N	O	P	Q	R
S	T	U	V	W	X	Y	Z	

Chapter 5: Personality Number Interpretations

Your pet's personality number comes from the sum of all the letters in their name.

Let's learn how to break down a name (Pythagorean Number System) and add it up.

EXAMPLE 1: LUCY

L=3, **U**=3, **C**=3, **Y**=7

Add the numbers and simplify them into one number

- ✓ 3+3+3+7
- ✓ 3+3 = 6, 3+7 =10
- ✓ 6+10 = 16
- ✓ The name Lucy adds up to the number 16
- ✓ 16 needs to be reduced to a single digit
- ✓ 1+6 = 7

The name Lucy is a 7 personality number

EXAMPLE 2: TITAN

T=2, **I**=9, **T**=2, **A**=1, **N**=5

Add the numbers

- ✓ 2+9+2+1+5
- ✓ 2+9 = 11, 2+1+5 = 8
- ✓ 11+8 = 19
- ✓ 19 needs to be reduced to a single digit
- ✓ 1+9 = 10
- ✓ 10 needs to be reduced to a single digit
- ✓ 1+0 = 1

The name Titan is a 1 personality number

Now do this for your pet's name and check below for their personality number interpretation.

ONE PETS:

Active, independent and loves to do what they want. Natural leaders but not good followers so be ready for some battles of wills. A one pet will run you and your household if you let them so stand your ground and be patient. If you want to show your pet, the one vibration will do well in competition. They love the spotlight and will not shy away from the camera. One pets are very protective of their family (pack) and will intuitively know if something is wrong. Excellent number name for a watch dog. Avoid a one name for cats and especially Siamese cats. Cats with the one vibration are extremely independent and may run away.

<u>**Health:**</u>
One's may be more prone to have problems related to stress, nausea, fevers, digestive system, eyes, and teeth.

One Name Examples:
Arco, Buck, Chewy, Ivan, Klaus, Minnie, Link, Navi, Roxy, Tank, Woody, Yari

TWO PETS:

Loving, affectionate, intuitive, stubborn, people oriented and very loyal. A two pet loves the outdoors and like to mark their territory. This pet will easily become your best friend and instinctively sense your moods and feelings. A two pet dislikes chaos, unnecessary clutter or disharmony. Excellent number name for pets that participate in shows or competitions.

Health:
Healthy appetite and likes to lie around so regular exercise is a must to prevent obesity and possible cardiovascular problems. May be prone to jaw and mouth issues.

Two Name Examples:
Agbar, Cinnamon, Dax, Gypsy, Hanna, Kato, Marley, Morris, Prince, Rugar

THREE PETS:

Friendly, playful, intelligent people loving pets who like to be close with their owners. This vibration loves to eat, meet new people, and experience new places. They tend to be amusing party animals who will make you laugh at their antics. In training they may appear indifferent but will perform when you least expect it. The three vibration is a good protector, needs a lot of attention and loves to be spoiled. Females are more extroverted than males. This number tends to have separation anxiety when left alone and will become very distressed if "locked" up.

Health:
Three pets are prone to liver problems and throw up easily. Avoid greasy food and table scraps. Youngsters will tend to chew and eat

anything and everything they can find so you have been warned.

Three Name Examples:
Argus, Gunther, Jagger, Lux, Roxi, Rusty, Sasha, Tabbie, Uri, Yogi

FOUR PETS:

These pets need to feel safe and thrive on routine. If something unexpected occurs this vibration gets cranky and their reactions can be unpredictable. These pets have an internal clock so it is important to keep meals, playtime and walks on a consistent schedule. Their home is very important to them and they are protective of it and you. Female fours are usually smarter than males. This pet will not hide their feeling for people or things they dislike. The four numbers makes good guard dogs, race horses and rodeo animals.

Health:
Four pets need to be exercised daily and have their diet strictly monitored as they have a tendency to gain weight. Stomach tends to be the fragile part of their bodies.

Four Name Examples:
Athena, Bane, Clyde, Fancy, Josie, Kiki, Lola, Moose, Nitro, Queenie, Socks

FIVE PETS:

A playful energy that is always ready for a walk or play. These pets are fast learners who adapt quickly to new environments and like having people around them. They are natural wanders and want a lot of freedom to explore. Unlike the four pet, the five pet craves variety. It can be challenging to control these pet's whereabouts as they do not like to be restrained or confined. Females tend to be more curious and sociable than males.

Health:
Five pets are active and need regular exercise. They may be prone to sudden fevers and cardiovascular problems.

Five Name Examples:
Aldo, Asta, Bella, Boomer, Duke, Emma, King, Lex, Lexi, Tabby

SIX PETS:

Caring, docile, family oriented, protective, very patient and a people pleaser. This vibration makes great service animals and is naturally tuned into their owners and families (pack). A six pet considers themselves an important member of the household and will appreciate you treating them as one. Females tend to be loving, better balanced, and calmer than males. Both genders may become insecure if they do not have a lot of affection or a tranquil environment.

Health:
Six pets will eat anything so they need balanced nutrition. Avoid lavishing them with too many treats. They may be prone to lymphatic problems.

Six Name Examples:
Axel, Blitz, Enzo, Greta, Haley, Hugo, Lady, Macy, Pepe, Winston

SEVEN PETS:

Attentive, friendly, observant, and the philosophers of the animal kingdom. The seven vibration is an easygoing, loving pet. They tend to be a loner at times so be sure to give them their space when needed. Though these pets need space, they also need your company more than they let on. Their behavior can become unpredictable if they are not getting enough attention. Females tend to be more irritable than males.

Health:
Seven pets need a low calorie diet. The bladder tends to be the weakest part of their body.

Seven Name Examples:
Bruno, Chloe, Fitz, Gunner, Hazel, Hoss, Jack, Otto, Rosco, Tails

EIGHT PETS:

Affectionate, docile, fast learners, good leaders, good guards, sweet and stubborn. This pet is often an exceptional looking animal and expects the best you have to offer. They enjoy the finer things in life and may turn up their noses at generic food, toys, etc. When your back is turned, the eight pet will ignore rules and help themselves to your cozy bed or the plush couch. Eight pets may pull mischievous stunts just to stir up some excitement when they find themselves bored or frustrated. An eight vibration will keep you on your toes. Females are mellower than males.

Health:
These pets need exercise to control their stress. Back legs and joints are the fragile parts in their body.

Eight Name Examples:
Bo, Boots, Gaby, Hitchcock, Leah, Merlin, Paxton, Roxie, Starlee, Titus, Zeus

NINE PETS:

Anxious, docile, friendly, intuitive, jealous, very loving and protective of their family (pack). The nine vibrations tend to have an "old soul" quality about them. They need a lot of love and will generally attach to one person. If they feel they are not getting enough attention, they will do whatever it takes to get it from you. This pet hates to be left alone so it would be wise to have more than one pet so there is always companionship. Females tend to be needier than males.

Health:

Can be prone to depression. Be sure you lavish this pet with a lot of attention and love. Tend to have poor digestive systems.

Nine Name Examples:

Aaros, Capone, Coco, Fergi, Hudson, Luxor, Nutters, Pixie, Rocco, Saber, Tess

Chapter 6: Master Numbers

ELEVEN PETS:

The eleven pet is a Master Number that "breaks down" into a two. Everything that applies to a two pet will apply to an eleven pet. The exception to the eleven pet is they are naturally psychic and will respond to their environment at a higher vibration.

TWENTY-TWO PETS:

A twenty-two pet "breaks down" into a four. Everything that applies to a four pet will apply to a twenty-two pet but at a higher vibration. A twenty-two pet is sensitive to change on a global level and may give subtle warnings before a natural disaster or medical condition strikes. A twenty-two pet is loyal and reliable and will appreciate you having the same qualities. It is possible that a twenty-two pet may have been with you in a previous life.

Chapter 7: Instinctive Reaction Number Interpretations

The number vibration of the first vowel of your pet's name will describe its instinctive reactions.

EXAMPLE: LUCY

    U=3

THE VALUE OF THE VOWELS:

A	E	I	O	U
1	5	9	6	3

Next, we need to know the meaning of each vowel as follows:

Vowel	INSTINCTIVE REACTIONS Meaning of the first vowel of a name.
A	Impulsive, independent, intelligent, anxious, outgoing, active and alert.
E	Intelligent, high spirited, lively, and runaway tendencies. Sometimes they can be nervous, and usually very playful.
I	Friendly, docile, devoted, loyal, affectionate, and need a harmonious environment to thrive. They don't like harsh words or yelling.
O	Loving, jealous, active, easygoing nature, and fond of their family. Their home is their world.
U	Joyful, smart, sociable, graceful, guarding instincts and children oriented.

Exceptions:

Names like Sylvia, the letter Y sounds like I. In this case, replace the Y with an I, which is the number NINE. The same is true for any other name where a letter sounds like a vowel. Play around with this and don't over analyze and get stressed. This is supposed to be fun!

Just remember, animals have a very acute sense of hearing.

* I have listed the charts together at the very end of the book for easy reference.*

BONUS CHAPTER: ASTROLOGY AND YOUR PET

Astrology and Numerology are the twin sciences that can be thought of as the two sides of one coin.

The science of astrology is based on stars and planets. To have an accurate astrological chart reading involves complicated calculations derived from the planetary positions of the sun, stars and moon as they were at the time and date of a birth.

Most of us do not have this information for our pets so the information below may not be precisely scientific but it is interesting and fun.

Look at the characteristics that apply to your pet's astrological sign and compare it with your pet's temperament, personality and health.

If you know the astrological sign of a "soon to be" pet, pay attention the numerological value of their name. Apply what you have learned in this book to avoid undesirable behaviors, vibrations and personality.

ARIES (The Ram) - March 21 to April 20

<u>Behavior</u> – Aries pets are generally very active and known to be anxious and nervous. They are hypersensitive to the environment around them but are also soft hearted. They need a lot of exercise

to burn off their nervous energy.

Health – May be prone to fever, ear and teeth problems.

Numerology – Avoid number 1 names and first vowel "A".

TAURUS (The Bull) - April 21 to May 21

Behavior – Taurus pets are faithful and family oriented. They have a passive nature about them but if they need to defend themselves or family members in a fight, they do not cower and they do not give up before a result is reached.

Health – May have difficulties chewing, may be susceptible to throat and ear infections.

Numerology – For a tranquil pet find names that end in 2, and first vowel "O".

GEMINI (The Twins) - May 22 to June 21

Behavior – Gemini pets are active, energetic, playful, good eaters, and great hunters. They socialize very easily with humans and other pets. Gemini pets tend to be extremely intelligent and quick learners therefore making it easy to train them. Their intelligence also means they can require a lot of attention to keep them out of mischief. They enjoy the company of their owners and relish lots of attention.

Health – May have problems in their legs.

Numerology – Avoid number 1 and 5 names, and first vowels "A" and "E".

CANCER (The Crab) - June 22 to July 23

Behavior – Cancer pets are family oriented, gentle, joyful and extremely sensitive. If they are mistreated, they will react with sadness. They do not get attached to a person easily but when they do, they are loyal for life. They hate being left alone.

Health – Problems with their stomach. They may vomit if food is not well digested.

Numerology – In order to decrease the cancerian pets' moodiness, avoid choosing number 4 names and first vowel "I".

LEO (The Lion) - July 24 to August 23

Behavior – Leo pets tend to be very independent, confident and are born leaders. They are difficult to train because they will fight you for alpha status. They are natural hams and love the spotlight. Even though they are independent they do not like to be alone. Leo pets expect compliments, massages, and all the pampering and attention you can give them.

Health – Avoid stress and anxiety. They may develop heart problems.

Numerology – Avoid number 1 and 5 names, and first vowels "A" and "E".

VIRGO (The Virgin) - August 24 to September 21

Behavior – Virgo pets have a multitude of characteristics and behaviors that make them wonderful human companions.

Health – Intestinal problems and subject to worms.

Numerology – Avoid number 4 names and first vowel "A".

LIBRA (The Scales) - September 22 to October 23

Behavior – Libra pets are extremely easygoing and people oriented. They are playful and everyone loves them. They hate being alone. They are fantastic pets for families that are not very active. Libra pets are typically somewhat lazy and need to be forced to exercise or they will eventually become overweight.

Health – Always take care of their nutrition and make sure that they drink water.

Numerology – Choose number 2 names, and first vowels "U" and "O" to reinforce all good qualities of your Libra pet.

SCORPIO (The Scorpion) - October 24 to November 23

Behavior – Scorpion pets are beautiful and usually have a nice coat. Scorpion pets can be jealous and extremely possessive of their owners. This typically makes for an extremely loyal pet but it can become a problem if the pet believes their owner is being threatened when they are not. They can be overprotective at times.

Health – Subject to skin allergies, so beware of perfumes and soaps. They are also sensitive to strong odors.

Numerology – Avoid number 7 and 9 names, and first vowel "I".

SAGITTARIUS (The Archer/Centaur) - November 24 to December 22

Behavior – Sagittarius pets are beautiful, playful and very friendly. They are fast learners and make great pets because they are fun loving and very intelligent. Because of their wonderful nature they are loved by all. However, their energy level can be difficult for individuals or families that are not used to active pets.

Health – Subject to circulatory and hip problems.

Numerology – Seek names ending in number 3, 5, and 8 names, and first vowels "U" and "O".

CAPRICORN (The Sea-Goat) - December 23 to January 21

Behavior – Capricorn pets are stubborn and can be moody. They have tender hearts and usually get attached to the person who treats them the best. Capricorn pets tend to remain very young at heart, and remain very playful even into their old age.

Health – Subject to joint problems.

Numerology – Seek number 2, 3, and 5 names, and first vowel "A", "E", and "I".

AQUARIUS (The Water-Carrier) - January 22 to February 19

Behavior – Aquarius pets are dynamic, sociable and playful. They are extremely intelligent. Their intelligence can come across as a level of stubbornness that makes them appear ill-tempered and sometimes difficult to handle. They need to be with people.

Health – Subject to circulatory, spine, and thigh problems.

Numerology – Choose number 3 and 5 names, and first vowels "E" and "U".

PISCES (The Fish) - February 20 to March 20

Behavior – Pisces pets are very introverted and extremely gentle and very sensitive to people around them. This pet is a good match for people who are naturally calm and easy going but not ideal for people who can be very emotional. Their calm nature makes them suitable for families.

Health – May be susceptible to problems in their paws and lymphatic system. Also may be subjected to ingesting poisons and be sensitive to drugs.

Numerology – Avoid number 2, 4 and 9 names, and first vowel "A", "E", and "I".

MEET THE AUTHOR

Amy & Bruno

Amy Morford has over twenty years of dog training experience with companion dogs, sport dogs and working breeds. Amy's motivation to write about dogs stems from her love for them and their unbiased loyalty and devotion. Amy's goal is to provide helpful, accurate information to assist dog lovers with raising and training a well-mannered, good-tempered, happy, healthy, well-adjusted companion, friend, partner and/or family pet.

Amy wrote this book out of love and affection for her canine students. She enjoys assisting pet lovers in every way possible; including helping them choose the best name for their pet or pets using the ancient system of numerology.

MORE BOOKS BY AMY MORFORD

DoggyPedia: All You Need To Know About Dogs

Dog Eldercare: Caring For Your Middle-Aged To Older Dog (Dog Care for the Older Canine)

Dog Quotes: Proverbs, Quotes & Quips

How to Speak Dog: Dog Training Simplified For Dog Owners

Puppy Training: From Day 1 to Adulthood (How to Make Your Puppy Loving and Obedient)

Scared Dog Audio

The German Shepherd Big Book: All About The German Shepherd Breed

Charts

PYTHAGOREAN NUMBER SYSTEM

1	2	3	4	5	6	7	8	9
A	B	C	D	E	F	G	H	I
J	K	L	M	N	O	P	Q	R
S	T	U	V	W	X	Y	Z	

THE VALUE OF THE VOWELS:

A	E	I	O	U
1	5	9	6	3

Vowel	INSTINCTIVE REACTIONS Meaning of the first vowel of a name.
A	Impulsive, independent, intelligent, anxious, outgoing, active and alert.
E	Intelligent, high spirited, lively, and runaway tendencies. Sometimes they can be nervous, and usually very playful.
I	Friendly, docile, devoted, loyal, affectionate, and need a harmonious environment to thrive. They don't like harsh words or yelling.
O	Loving, jealous, active, easygoing nature, and fond of their family. Their home is their world.
U	Joyful, smart, sociable, graceful, guarding instincts and children oriented.

www.ingramcontent.com/pod-product-compliance
Lightning Source LLC
LaVergne TN
LVHW012057070526
838200LV00070BA/1935